HUSTLING WITH GOD

Phase 1:

From Nothing To Something

Author

Wayne Lee

Hustling With God

ISBN 978-1-7344446-1-2 (Paperback Edition)

The intent of the author is only to offer information of a general nature to help you in your quest for spiritual well-being. In the event, you use any of the information in this book for yourself, which is your constitutional right, the author and the publisher assume no responsibility for your actions.

Unless otherwise indicated, all Scripture quotations are from the King James Version of the Bible.

Cover photo taken by C.B.3 Photography

Front, Spine, & Back Cover by Matasha Lee

First publishing February 2020

@gottamakit

Table of Contents

DEDICATION

This book is dedicated to those who feel they are worth more than they currently have...

PREFACE

Faith is the belief in things that you cannot see.

It was an early Saturday morning, after a late-night of, "Who can stay up the longest?" Between me, my wife, our two boys, and the host of nieces and nephews that we had sleeping over. Even though I was one of the first ones to see the back of my eyelids that night. That morning, I was the first one to rise because I wanted to seize the opportunity, to share with my son's, a glance of how my sleepovers use to be, When my father would wake up early and have the aroma of breakfast being prepared, passing from room to room.

After discovering that our cupboard wasn't prepared for ten guests. I decided to make a store run to the local grocery store and there is where I discovered, the purpose of my growing testimony.

In a world that's going through so many different changes, with the increase of modern-day technology. I begin to recognize, that my efforts to show my children, a glance of what my childhood was like, was going to be one of the few glances from my childhood that they will ever see. Because when I was growing up, inside of this local grocery store, there use to be a host of cashiers manning the registers and ready to greet the incoming shoppers for the early morning rush.

In the year of 2019, it is no longer like that. Inside of this very same grocery store, there is now only one person and a host of self-checkout lines that will greet you accordingly to the time of day.

As I stood next in line, I couldn't help but to feel the hopelessness of former cashiers, When they were told that their services would no longer be needed. In that moment, that's when I knew that my testimony could be a light for others. For I have walked the path of being no longer needed and not to have a clue on what to do next. I know what it's like, to see the holidays fast approaching and not have a way to provide for your loved ones. I feel it's now safe to say that I have looked into the eyes of my financial struggles and have overcome them, but I didn't do it alone.

This book is a representation of my walk with God and the light that God has revealed to me, on how to come out of the cycle of not having and into the cycle of having.

My mission within the pages of this book, is not to bring about a newfound belief system but to raise the level of awareness to something we are already a master at doing... Creating!!!

MY TESTIMONY

Hustling is the art of going from nothing to something. By using one's desire, creativity and effort.

*"People don't hide a lamp under a bowl. They put it on a lampstand. Then the light shines for everyone in the house."... **Matthew 5:15 ERV***

The biggest improvement I ever made in my life, Was the day I asked God to show me how to hustle because in that moment, God responded to me with two words, "Try Faith!"

Hallelujah, I'm so glad I tried faith!!!

Because before adding God to my hustle, I was struggling mightily with the responsibilities of being an Adult. For my roles in life were multiplying, but my paycheck in life was remaining the same.

8

Along my journey through life, I've traveled down many different paths. Seeking opportunities to increase my earnings, but after so long, everything and anything that I tried, always seemed to lead me back into the same situation of struggling to get by. Oftentimes, I would find myself blaming God for seemingly not rewarding me for my efforts, but that all changed the day I realized. I have never once asked God, "What should I be doing to make money!?!"

I am ashamed to admit this now, but in all honesty, I use to think that God's ONLY concern was with us getting into Heaven after we die, and since you can't take money with you, I figured money and God didn't belong in the same sentence. Wow, was I so wrong, and I am not ashamed to admit that!

One of the first things that I discovered, after inviting God into my hustle and may very well be the greatest revelation that I've experienced up to this point in my life, is that God WANTS me to be rewarded for the amount of faith, that I put into my hustle (Romans 12:3).

See God knew, from the moment of our inception, that we were heading into a world, where money was going to play a huge role in our individual lives. So with that knowing and while we were still forming in our mother's womb. God placed within us all, our very own set of divine gifts. Gifts that we are able to tap into from various entry-level points (faith), to formulate (think) and create (hustle) the type of money (worth) we desire to have in our individual lives.

With that newfound outlook on God and my life. I begin to humble myself, by laying down the vision that I had over my life and asked God for a better vision for my life (Matthew 10:39).

I remember acknowledging to God, "That you know me better then I know myself. You who knows even the smallest of details about me, such as the count of hairs on top of my head (Luke 12:7). Surely you must know the best route for me to take when it comes to producing a more desirable income! Will you show me through a Christian point of view, how to best use the gifts that you blessed me with, to create the type of hustle, that will allow me to have the type of money that I desire to have? A hustle that will not only provide me with the funds but along with it, the type of peace, joy, and love that surpasses all of my understanding!"

By letting go of my own vision and choosing the vision that God showed me for my life. I began to wake up to the fact that if God created me and everything within the Earth. Then it's possible that God can show me how to best use my own set of divine gifts, to bring about the wealth that's been set aside for me since the beginning of time (Romans 8:29).

My inspiration behind writing this book, is to let you know that your dreams are real and that your dreams are meant to come true! (1 Peter 1:4)

I wrote this book to show you, how God can take a gift that you may see as useless and allow everything that you ever dreamed of to flow from it.

I wrote this book for the individuals, who may be like myself, that didn't see the type of success they envisioned, with Dream #1 or Dream #2. This book is to remind you, of how good God is and that the mistakes that you keep seeming to make and those setbacks that you keep seeming to have, are all leading you to an amazing place in your life. For there's a blessing to be gained, through every struggle, if only we don't give up! For the pitfalls and challenges, we endure, create within us a space of desire, and that desire is the beginning of all things (Luke 12:31).

I'm talking to the person, that desires to provide for their family in a way that they always dreamed of doing. Yes, it's still possible for you! I'm talking to the person, that desires to change their life for the better. Yes, it's still possible for you! I'm talking to the Bosses, who currently works for someone else but desires to start up their own companies, so that others may be given an opportunity for employment. Yes, it's still possible for you!

I know this to be true, for I have once dreamed of these things to happen in my life and I am blessed to say that, "I have brought a portion of Heaven to Earth, through the Grace that God provides and I am now living in a reality, that I once only dreamed of!"

Here is my truth on what Faith can do. I pray that through my life's journey, you will gain something that will help benefit you along your life's journey!

Welcome to Phase 1: From nothing to something...
Enjoy!

WORDS OF WISDOM
NEVER UNDERESTIMATE THE POWER OF YOUR
TESTIMONY.... CHRISTINE CAINE

INTRODUCTION

How Do You See The World?

A Viewpoint is the position from which something or someone is observed.

*"For my thoughts are not your thoughts, neither are your ways my ways, saith the Lord. For as the heavens are higher than the earth, so are my ways higher than your ways, and my thoughts than your thoughts."... **Isaiah 55:8-9 KJV***

Isn't it amazing, how two people can be in the same place, seeing and hearing the same thing but yet be able to walk away with two totally different opinions on what took place?

What's even more amazing, is that in any given situation, both of their opinions can be considered to be the right opinion to have.

Have you ever wondered why!?!

14

The reason behind this amazing social phenomenon is due to one's own chosen viewpoint of the world. For when a person looks through the lens of a particular viewpoint, they impregnate a mindset that gives birth to the amount of faith an individual has. Faith that goes on to give birth to thoughts, thoughts that then give birth to words. Words that then give birth to visions, visions that then give birth to actions. Actions that then give birth to results and those results, end up creating the world around them, thus justifying one's own chosen viewpoint. In other words, each viewpoint leads down its own path and lands at it's own destiny.

Case in point, let's take me at two different times in my life, after being told that my services were no longer needed at a place of employment.

When it happen to me the first time, I immediately went out and sought a job that would pay me the same amount of wages that my previous employer had paid me. For that was the Viewpoint that I had for myself. I felt I deserved to be paid the same amount because I desired to continue to live, the same type of lifestyle that I had at the time.

With that chosen viewpoint of myself, it released within me the amount of faith required to start at that level of pay. Mind you; I'm going back into an unemployment world that presents many different levels of pay and opportunity. Ranging from minimum wage and beyond. With the chosen viewpoint of earning the same level of income, I did not once consider, going backwards to apply for a minimum wage job because my viewpoint presented a greater amount of faith in myself. Nor did I ever apply for a wage greater than I previously had, for my viewpoint did not release the amount of faith required to go to the next level and beyond. So to make a long story short, I ended up landing a job in the area of the amount of faith that I had for myself.

On my second go around, after being told that my services were no longer needed at a place of employment. I took on a different approach, as I was heading back into the unemployment world. For I had chosen a new viewpoint for myself. No longer did I feel like I desired to have a job that produced the same level of income. I felt I deserved more! So I chose to have a viewpoint of myself earning "much more," which then gave birth to the amount of faith required to go after the positions that paid "much more." Faith that then allowed me to start thinking in terms of having "much more." Thinking that allowed me to start talking to myself about obtaining "much more." Talking that allowed me to start seeing myself having "much more," and when I started seeing myself having "much more." I began to make moves in a way that fulfilled how I saw myself. Moves that started getting the type of results that were in line with my faith. Thus justifying my newfound viewpoint, that I had chosen for myself.

So, in the case of two people (that are) not seeing eye to eye, when confronted with a similar situation. The only way for a person to truly understand the opinion of the other person is for one to allow their Viewpoint to be replaced in favor of the other person's viewpoint. For when we take on another person's viewpoint, we allow ourselves the opportunity to travel down a Viewpoint's path to see, hear, and understand the world that the other person is living in.

In that same manner, we are able to change our viewpoints, when our views of the world are no longer helping us live the lives we desire to live.

That is what the Lord is offering, when the Bible tells us, "My ways are higher than your ways, and my thoughts are higher than your thoughts!" God is presenting to us an invitation to have faith in something that's greater than ourselves!

WORDS OF WISDOM
IF YOU DON'T NEED GOD TO PULL OFF WHAT YOU ARE PLANNING, YOU ARE NOT DREAMING BIG ENOUGH.... MICHAEL HYATT

THE BLUEPRINT

A Blueprint is a design plan, which serves as a model of guidance in the form of a detailed plan or program of action.

"For I know the plans I have for you," declares the Lord, "plans to prosper you and not to harm you, plans to give you hope and a future."... **Jeremiah 29:11 NIV**

There aren't many things in this world that connects man with God; the way Hustling connects man with God. Since the beginning of time, the art of Hustling has served as the blueprint on how to go from nothing to something. For the art of Hustling, is unmatched in its ability to collaborate one's own mental (Heaven) capacity, with one's own physical (Earth) capacity. To bring about the existence, of what was once only foreseen, in one's own imagination (Romans 4:17).

God saw this narrative to be so important to and for mankind that from the opening pages of the Bible, God wasted no time revealing the blueprint on how to go from nothing (Heaven) to something (Earth).

Now Pause... Before we go any further, I want you to think about your dreams and what you desire to achieve in your life. Now keep it on your mind as we navigate through the blueprint on how to bring Heaven to Earth.

"In the beginning God created the heaven and the earth."... Genesis 1:1 KJV
By starting with nothing but just the desire to do so, God begins creating The Heavens and The Earth. The word 'create' means to produce through the imagination. *Note that God has not yet made the Heavens and the Earth, God has only went into the imagination and saw the desire as completed. Hence the word, created (past tense). **As a hustler, this teaches us to begin with the end goal in mind.

"And the earth was without form, and void; and darkness was upon the face of the deep. And the Spirit of God moved upon the face of the waters."... Genesis 1:2 KJV.

The earth without form, is an indication of no structure, no order nor plan of action in place. Void illustrates emptiness and nothingness, while darkness reveals the absence of light. In other words, God is revealing that at the beginning stages of creativity, the mind is in a state of chaos, for uncertainty is present. God is also revealing, that uncertainty is normal at this stage of the process. For this verse shows us that even God does not yet have an idea or a plan in place on how to merge the Heavens with the Earth. *Remember, thus-far God has only pictured (created) the end result. **Water in this verse represents faith (James 1:6) and the Spirit Of God is moving upon faith (water) gauging accordingly.

**Oftentimes, dreams die at this stage for lack of Faith. For we know what we want to accomplish but be completely lost on how to go about accomplishment. Just hold your water (faith), Help is on the way!

"And God said, Let there be light: and there was light."... Genesis 1:3 KJV
It's something about that water because after faith (water) was gauged, notice that God begins to speak for the first time. Saying 'let there be light.' Let means to free from. Ex. I let out a scream. There

means at that point or stage. Ex. Stop right there. Be means to exist, while the word Light represents a spiritual illumination; we call them ideas (flashbulb moment).

In other words, "According to the measure of faith one has in the moment of disorder and confusion (darkness). God freed (let) up an idea (light) from darkness, that was at the stage (there) of faith (water) presently available."

We must remember everything on earth once came out of darkness. From the materials that our homes are made out of, to the food that nurtures and grows our bodies. All things are formed out of darkness, and God's plan for your life is no exception.

*Note-God spoke light and then light begin to shine (process). When we begin to speak into the direction we desire to go, the way to get there (light) will reveal itself.

"And God saw the light, that it was good: and God divided the light from the darkness."... Genesis 1:4 KJV

God is now providing structure and order amongst the chaos. By separating the do's of light, from the darkness of don't's. *Note that when God saw the light, God also saw the light as good. Good means bountiful. Ex. That's good news. Good means fertile. Ex. That's some good land. Good means profitable. Ex. That's a good deal. God encouraged God, when no one else was around.

**Oftentimes, ideas die at this stage, from the lack of seeing the good in the idea that God has blessed us with. Glory to God, for the ability to see the good in things!

"And God called the light Day, and the darkness he called Night. And the evening and the morning were the first day."... Genesis 1:5 KJV
Take notes- What did God accomplish on the first day? Basically, God got God's mind right by creating a level of something to focus the mind on. Notice that God has not yet raised a finger to make anything. Not a piece of grass, not a mountain, not a man nor a woman. Creation is not done overnight, even for God, it's a process.

God said, Let there be a firmament in the midst of the waters, and let it divide the waters from the waters."... Genesis 1:6 KJV
*Note that God spoke again. Since water represents faith, God has now divided faith from faith. **I wanna tell you what a firmament is so bad,

but I'll let the scripture reveal itself. (I think it's better that way)

"And God made the firmament, and divided the waters which were under the firmament from the waters which were above the firmament: and it was so."... Genesis 1:7 KJV

*Note-God made something for the first time. Initially upon reading this verse, it may sound like a repeat of the previous verse. But what God is revealing, is the formula on how to bring about what was once only foreseen in the imagination (Heaven).

First said, then saw. Then made what was seen. "Through faith we understand that the worlds were framed by the word of God." (Hebrews 11:3) God is bringing to life the thing imagine, through speech.

"And God called the firmament Heaven. And the evening and the morning were the second day."... Genesis 1:8 KJV

*Note-God is passing out names now. Names are special because names bring about a certain nature in things.

Wow, so firmament is Heaven!

Now let's go back to the previous verse (Genesis 1:7), with our newfound knowledge... God made heaven and divided the faith which were under the heavens, from the faith which were above the heavens and it was so. **God has now created 2 different levels of faith, one that requires you to believe in yourself (Earthly Faith) and one that requires total faith in God to deliver (Heavenly Faith). *Note-Notice the level of focus that God has carried over from Day 1 to Day 2. God didn't get sidetracked; God picked up where God left off. **Distractions delay dreams.

"And God said, Let the waters under the heaven be gathered together unto one place, and let the dry land appear: and it was so."... Genesis 1:9 KJV
        *Note-God spoke, and it was so. As soon as we speak on something, it becomes real. Recognize it's not yet made, but yet it still exists. Now God has taken all the faith (water) that resides under the heaven and brought it all together and made it one.

Hold up, wait a minute; I knew it was something about that water!

In verse 6, when God divided the waters from the waters. You are telling me that's the same divide, that God uses to gauge the amount of light to shine from verse 3, from when God's Spirit was moving upon the face of the waters (faith) in verse 2... Wow, that's deep but good to know, and I'll give you a few reasons why...

#1 The portion of water (faith) that is in Heaven, was first a whole body of water (faith) on Earth, then the water (faith) was divided on Earth. Earth got its portion and Heaven got its portion. Meaning you already have a connection with your destiny (Heaven), before you ever get started!

#2 God is willing to use the dark places of your life to brighten the lights of your future.

#3 We also now know why all the waters (faith) are gathered into one place. For that is the amount of faith (water) that already existed within, when God took a look.

Okay we starting to get somewhere; bring forth the dry land!

"And God called the dry land Earth; and the gathering together of the waters called he Seas: and God saw that it was good."... Genesis 1:10 KJV

*Note-God has created a little bit more and stopped to give some encouragement along the way. "It's good!" Once again, God is establishing order by providing structure to the thoughts that are

forming. Once the light shined, it's clear that God has now fully embraced the given idea (light) and is no longer focusing on what still lies in the dark. But rather is showing faith through action.

That is encouraging because it also reveals to us that God is not concerned about the things we have done in the past (darkness). God's focus is on our light (future).

"And God said, Let the earth bring forth grass, the herb yielding seed, and the fruit tree yielding fruit after his kind, whose seed is in itself, upon the earth: and it was so."... Genesis 1:11 KJV

*Note-God has spoken again and it was so. Yielding means to produce. This verse is packed with so much power and revelation, but let's focus on "whose seed is in itself." In a apple seed is an apple tree. Within a child is an adult, that also was once a seed. Seeds are important, for that's how God delivers all things. Everything God gives us at first is in seed form. That's why faith (water) is so important. Faith yields (produces) the seed (desire).

Fruit tree yielding fruit after his kind. Is like an apple yielding (producing) apple juice, apple cider vinegar, apple pie, etc. In other words, within a single idea, yields (produces) many ideas of its kind. Empire State Of Mind!

*Note-The gifts that we have can operate on many different levels!

"And the earth brought forth grass, and herb yielding seed after his kind, and the tree yielding fruit, whose seed was in itself, after his kind: and God saw that it was good."... Genesis 1:12 KJV

   *Note-This time God has freed the earth to commit acts (Let The Earth). Once again, peep the formula. God said and it was so, and then things start shifting in order. **Once again, note the encouragement along the way. For The Earth and it's many wonders has not yet been fully created. So, for God to say it was good over and over again. It lets us know that the presence of "you ain't doing nothing," was there also. IT WAS GOOD!

"And the evening and the morning were the third day."... Genesis 1:13 KJV

   Throughout the rest of this chapter and throughout the rest of the Bible, as well. God continues to unveil the many blueprints, that instruct us on how to overcome and thrive against the many situations and circumstances that life may bring about.

For the purpose of Hustling and beginning with nothing at hand, we will focus on the first 3 days of creation (Genesis 1:1-13). For its within the first 3 days, that God has revealed to us the principles on how to re-energize and revive God's plan in our lives.

Yes, God has a plan in place, that's just waiting on your faith and your effort, to prosper you into new heights of financial success. The following pages will reveal to you, how you are able to align yourself with God's plan and bring to life the financial success you always imagined!

WORDS OF WISDOM
NOBODY BUILT LIKE YOU, YOU DESIGN YOURSELF.... JAY-Z

UNDERSTANDING DESIRE

Desire is the conscious impulse towards something that promises satisfaction in its attainment.

*"In the beginning God created the heaven and the earth."... **Genesis 1:1 KJV***

From a physical sense, throughout the Bible's first 3 days of creation. The word 'desire' is nowhere to be found, but the evidence of God's desire can be seen in every move that God made.

As a Hustler, the thing that I can appreciate the most about having God as the driving force behind my hustle, is how God uses every inch of my life, to mold and shape me in a way that prepares me for the road ahead.

See, when I first came to God and ask God to show me how to hustle. I was completely at a loss on which direction to go. For I felt I had already exhausted every opportunity that was available to me. In fact, the only thing that I had left to stand on was my faith in God and my desire to support my family without having to struggle through life to do so.

Now let me show you how God works!

A couple of days removed, from laying down the viewpoint that I had over my life and asking God for a better viewpoint for my life. I overheard a discussion on the radio, about how much money it will take, in order for a household in America to live comfortably...

Have you ever heard something and thought to yourself, I think they're talking to me!?! (Romans 10:17)

To me, it felt like bells and whistles just went to ringing and blowing. Needless to say, the conversation caught my attention, so as I continued to listen. One of the speakers mentioned, "That in the year of 2014 and beyond, it will take at least

$100K per household a year, to live comfortably in America".... Upon hearing that statement, I became fully aware of how much money it will take (worth), to fulfill my reason for hustling (family).

Now here is where the magic takes place because God has now done God's part, by providing the seed but it is not enough to just have the seed (word). We as individuals, must plant the seed within us by claiming those words as our very own. Either you believe it's for you (faith) or you don't (doubt)!

Now before we move on, take a moment to glance back over your life, as I make this bold statement about you. Each decision you ever made in the nature of Faith, took you to the next level of knowing something, while each decision you ever made with Doubt, shut down the whole operation and you were unable to take another step toward your destiny!

Now I can't tell you why I did it, nothing in my background said I could, I just said, "That's me now, I make $100K a year!" I chose Faith and claimed those words (seeds) as my very own.

At the time, you could say I was reaching because I was only making about $15K a year, which ain't even half of a $100K.

At the time, you could say I was reaching because no one else in my family had ever produced $100K a year before.

Yes, you could definitely say I was reaching because if you don't understand faith, everything will seem like a reach and impossible to achieve (Hebrews 11:6).

Now stay with me now because God is about to kick it into gear.

Let's recap, I started out with only my faith, that God was going to do something, and with the desire to support my family, in hopes of not having to struggle to do so. This then led me to the knowledge of how much money (worth) it will take to fulfill my desire. (Ecclesiastes 10:19)

Within the art of Hustling (creating), its essential to know the amount of money it will take (worth), to fully support the reason you hustle,

BEFORE you start hustling (creating). For the amount of money you desire to have, shapes the framework of your hustle. Within a framework is the opportunities you recognize, the people you meet, the lessons you learn, the level of work ethic you develop, and the knowledge that you discover. For it's as if God takes a line, that starts at your desired amount and draws it all the way back to your present moment. Creating circumstances and situations that ultimately lead you to your destination.

For example, a person that desires to make $10 an hour, will attract $10 an hour opportunities. Meaning they will attract people into their lives, that's producing $10 an hour, while attracting the type of circumstances that develop the work ethic of an individual that produces $10 an hour. They would never see the opportunity to make $100 an hour come their way because it's outside the framework of their hustle. More importantly, that person is showing God, that their level of faith in their hustle, is at $10 an hour and not at $100 an hour.

If you are not following me and are unable to see what has happened thus far, what God has done is take my Faith to whole new level (Romans 12:3). For when your faith grows, your possibilities (thinking) grow with it.

#1 God replaced the thoughts of not struggling, with the thoughts of living comfortably (in Peace)!
#2 God created in me, a higher desire of worth, by allowing me to hear what it takes to fulfill my desire!
#3 God transition me from thinking check to check, to in terms of a yearly income!
CAN YOU SAY, INCREASE!!!

I have yet to produce a dime, but through my faith, God begins to mold and shape my way of thinking. That's important, for our thoughts become things, and my original way of thinking was not creating the type of income I desired to have. If so, I would have had it already.

Our why aligns us with our desire.

In order to create effectively, we must first identify within ourselves, what's being desired (not struggle/Earth) and the purpose (family/Heaven) behind the desire because that then lets us know (light), what to create (peace/Earth) and to what level ($100K/Heaven) it shall be created to.

God's desire was to create both a heaven and a earth and not just one or the other. The purpose behind it, was to let us know that Heaven (purpose) and Earth (desire) are both compatible with each other. In our case, that's a rendezvous of both purpose (Heaven) and desire (Earth), activated through a starting place called imagination (God). <u>For where there are two or more gathered in my name, there I will be also (Matthew 18:20)</u>.

The bringing together of Heaven (purpose) and Earth (desire), is what provoked God's spirit to begin to move in Genesis 1:2.

To fully grasp the blessing that's being sent through our desires, let's breakdown the word 'desire' and unpack the mystery of how the beginning of things form.

The prefix of desire is de-, which means to remove from. Like, dethrone and detached. The suffix of desire is -sire, which means male ancestor and/or originator. The origin of the word desire comes from the Latin word 'sidus,' which means heavenly body. Now bring (de-) and (-sire) back together, and we now know that the conscious impulse that we call desire, is a feeling that's "removed from the originator." In other words, our true desires come from God, which is in Heaven (Philippians 2:13 NLT). That's why in Proverbs 4:23, the Bible tells us, "Above all else, guard your heart, for everything you do flows from it!"

How we take in and see God's desire, determines the course of our lives and faith is the power that moves desire from Heaven (mind) to Earth (body) and into our Reality! Be mindful of what you are desiring....

God uses our desire to make ways out of no way!

Now here comes the amazing part. As our desire begins to take shape, step one of God's blueprint begins to take shape as well. That is what God is showing us in Genesis 1:1, to see the end in the beginning.

SCRIPTURES TO FIGHT WITH:

"Seek ye the kingdom of God; and all these things shall be added unto you." *Luke 12:31 KJV*

"So then faith cometh by hearing, and hearing by the word of God." *Romans 10:17 KJV*

"For God is working in you, giving you the desire and the power to do what pleases him." *Philippians 2:13 NLT*

*"A feast is made for laughter, and wine maketh merry: but money answereth all things." **Ecclesiastes 10:19 KJV***

UNDERSTANDING DARKNESS

Darkness is a place or time of little or no understanding.

"And the earth was without form, and void; and darkness was upon the face of the deep. And the Spirit of God moved upon the face of the waters."... Genesis 1:2 KJV

As we take on the natural transition, that flows us from one place to another. We arrive at a place in God's blueprint (Genesis 1:2), known as uncertainty. For this is the place that God described in so many words, as chaotic. A space of utter confusion and disorder. The site of darkness, where one can easily lose sight of their own way. The ultimate battlegrounds! As Hustlers, we must learn to master the battlefield of darkness, for this is ground zero. The place where our faith will be measured, and our worth will be determined.

The key to survival at this stage in the process of creating is to know that the battle is not yours to fight but that it is God's battle (blind faith). For the Bible tells us that it was God's Spirit that was moving upon the face of the waters and not we ourselves (Genesis 1:2).

When I first claimed (created) the viewpoint of earning a $100K a year (desire). I begin to notice that the outlook of my present circumstance was beginning to create mirrors of doubt within my psyche (darkness). For I was visualizing myself living one way on the inside of me but on the outside of me, I was going through something totally different (without form). Not to mention the fact that I was unemployed and was producing far less than the amount of money that I envisioned myself having (void)...

The battles we face on this particular battlefield, is not one of nutrition but of one of capacity. The capacity to have the faith, to see our world through the lens of our new viewpoint, while being surrounded in the reality of our former viewpoint.

Within the 14th chapter of the book of Exodus, the Bible gives us a great illustration of what our minds are going through, as we transition out of a former viewpoint and into a new viewpoint.

The story picks up, as the Pharaoh of Egypt (present circumstance) has just decided to release the children of Israel (our mind) from the hands of bondage (former viewpoint). As the children of Israel set out on their journey to reach the Promised Land (new viewpoint). The Pharaoh then decides to have a change of heart and goes after the children of Israel (our mind), so that they may be brought back into the hands of bondage (former viewpoint). As the Pharaoh draws near, the children of Israel (our mind) begin to have doubt in their decision to leave Egypt (former viewpoint). For they were starting to feel that it was better to live a life of bondage than to die in the wilderness (uncertainty). But in the midst of their doubt, there was a man named Moses (faith) that urged the children of Israel (our mind) to continue to move forward (new viewpoint), for God was on their side and will fight their battle. When the children of Israel (our mind) turned their sights from what the Pharaoh (present circumstance) was doing and continued to move forward in faith. God then responded to their act of faith, by parting the Red Sea (darkness) and allowing the children of Israel (our mind) to pass through to the other side (light). But that didn't stop the Pharaoh (present circumstance) from chasing after them. The Pharaoh attempted to pass through the divide of the Red Sea as well but was unable to reach the other side. For God closed back the divide of the Red Sea, and the Pharaoh (present circumstance) was no more.

At first glance, darkness can look like the worst enemy a dream can have, and it can be if we continue to look through the lens of our present circumstance (former viewpoint). But darkness can also serve as a friend rather than a foe when we choose to look through the lens of our fulfilled desire (new viewpoint). For that's faith at it's finest. The ability to focus on what is to come, instead of focusing on what is (Genesis 1:3). Whatever we focus on, we tend to replay over and over again inside our heads (imagination). By choosing to have faith in something greater then our present circumstance, we give God the authority to clear the path ahead, so that we may enter into the light (new viewpoint) that brings us out of darkness (former viewpoint).

I can admit, choosing to have faith blindly, is not always the easiest thing to do. For there's a reason why I'm not writing about the million-dollar experience or the billion-dollar opportunity that God presented before me. For God has shown me those amazing possibilities as well but the truth is, during those times, I did not see myself in Step 2 (darkness) as God showed me in Step 1 (desire).

See lack of faith can come in many forms, such as thinking you're not talented enough or not smart enough to get the job done. That's when we must remember that our fight is not against flesh and blood. Rather that's with our own flesh or against others but that our fight is with the way that we view things (Ephesians 6:12).

As Hustlers, it is vital that we master the space of darkness, for there are levels to the things we do and each level comes with its own layer of darkness to overcome. The good news is that each time we reach the light, we gain more and more faith (confidence) that we will come out of darkness and into the light, the next time around as well. The hard part is, getting over that initial space of darkness, and that's when the beauty of the Bible comes into play.

The thing that is so special about the Bible is that the Bible is written in a way that conforms to your way of thinking. Meaning how you come to the Bible, is a direct correlation to what you get from the Bible. If you come at the Bible with the intent of getting into heaven in your afterlife, that's the seed of evidence you're going to reap. If you come at the Bible, with the intent of seeing the Bible as lies and deceit, that's the seed of evidence you're going to reap. If you come at the Bible, with the intent of gaining insight on how to increase your value and worth in life, that's also the seed of evidence you're going to reap. For that's the beauty of the Bible, whatever you are going through, no matter the subject. The wisdom and knowledge on how to overcome the matter is within its pages!

After developing that level of understanding, I begin to approach the Bible as if it is my own personal Owners Manual. Take a vehicle for example, for the most part all vehicles come with an owner's manual. Vehicles typically come with an owner's manual because within its pages, is the knowledge of how to operate that particular vehicle to its fullest potential. Now you don't have to necessarily use the owner's manual to operate the vehicle, but the owner's manual is there and available to you to help you achieve optimum use.

I remember this one time, when I should of read my car's owners manual first before I ever started driving this one car that I had purchased. For it was my first car that required diesel fuel, and I was unaware of that. I ended up pumping regular gas inside the car, and as a result, I messed up my whole engine. I now try my best to read the owner's manual first, for everything that I buy.

I brought that experience to light because after reading the Bible with the intent of increasing my worth in life. I discovered that I was going about my life the wrong way. Don't get me wrong, I was living and having what I thought to be success, in a lot of areas of my life, but after reading the Bible with the intent to increase my worth (money). I became aware that I was not operating in my fullest potential.

Through the words and the stories that the Bible provides, I begin to realize that I was capable of so much more. Which then led me to thinking differently about myself, seeing myself differently, speaking to myself differently (inner voice), and, as a result, living differently.

You will discover that when you choose to have faith during moments of darkness (doubt). The doubt (darkness) that's within you, will begin to fade, as your faith (light) begins to grow into the next stage of its evolution. For your mind (God) will begin projecting various ways (gifts), on how to draw yourself nearer to the thing in which you desire to have, even while you are still in the midst of being in your present circumstance.

To give you a modern-day example of how this looks, within the world that we live in today... While I was choosing to have Faith in my worth (desire) of making $100K a year, in spite of what my present circumstance of being unemployed was showing me. The opportunity to get a Commercial Drivers License, seem to start popping up everywhere. It was on tv commercials, billboards, ads on my mailbox, etc. etc. At the time, I was unaware that God was leading me in that direction, but when I think back from where I was to now. That's exactly what God was doing! For I had the divine gift to drive within me the whole time but the potential of what my gift could produce, was lying dormant inside of me because I had never before, matched my level of faith, with the level of what I was desiring to produce ($100K a yr). That's why the

Bible reminds us that without faith, it is impossible to please God (our minds).

You can always tell when God is about to part the Red Sea of your dark place because the way you begin to see your opportunities (light), begins to match up with the worth (new viewpoint) that you have been desiring to produce.

WORDS OF WISDOM
FOR EVERY DARK NIGHT, THERE'S A BRIGHTER DAY.... TUPAC

SCRIPTURES TO FIGHT WITH:

"And ye shall know the truth, and the truth shall make you free." *John 8:32*

"For where two or three are gathered together in my name, there am I in the midst of them." *Matthew 18:20 KJV*

"But without faith it is impossible to please him: for he that cometh to God must believe that he is, and that he is a rewarder of them that diligently seek him." *Hebrews 11:6 KJV*

"For we wrestle not against flesh and blood, but against principalities, against powers, against the rulers of the darkness of this world, against spiritual wickedness in high places." *Ephesians 6:12 KJV*

UNDERSTANDING LIGHT

Light is something that makes vision possible.

"And God saw the light, that it was good: and God divided the light from the darkness."... **Genesis 1:4 KJV**

"**I**ndescribable!"... That's often the reply of first-time parents, when they are asked, "What is it like, to be a Mother or a Father now?"

When you come into the light (idea) of something you and God put together, the feeling can also be described as indescribable. For you have now personally witnessed how faith can move in your life, from what you once saw as only a dream (desire), now begins to give birth to ideas (light), that are specifically designed for the way God made you!

49

As hustlers, we call this having our own lane and ain't nothing like being in your own lane, with God at the wheel. For God not only knows the depths of our potential but also the best way to bring that potential out of us.

The key to survival at this stage in the process of creating is to have the faith that your light (idea) is good and that it is meant to work for your good.

If you have been holding on to the faith in who you desire to be and still feel as if you are in the dark on how to be... First off, know that you have done nothing wrong and that feeling your way through the dark, is a normal part of the process. For what you are experiencing is how to walk by faith and not by sight.

...After the rush of excitement wore off, of creating a new viewpoint ($100K a year) over my life. I begin to notice that I was completely unaware of any jobs that produce an income of $100K a year (darkness). At the time, I was also unaware that I could have simply "google" jobs that produce $100K a year. So instead, I choose to do as my Creator would do, and I reimagined (created) myself already being in the space I desired to be in life (walking by faith).

I envisioned my family being together and in a peaceful place in our lives. I envisioned a refrigerator full of food and designer clothes on our backs. I envisioned cars in the driveway and money in our bank accounts, as if these things had already come to pass!

As days passed, the thought then came to my mind to google jobs that produced a $100K a yr.

Side Note: We are in the age of information, for the most part, whatever we desire to know is at the tip of our fingertips (Use It!)...

When I googled jobs that produced a $100K a yr., I didn't see not one job that I qualified for, but I did see businesses that presented me with opportunity. There were several different types of businesses that could potentially produce my desired level of income, but the one that stood out for me was as an Independent Contractor driving 18-wheelers.

The reason it stood out to me is like I said at the end of the previous chapter. The opportunity to get a Commercial Drivers License was seemingly at every turn I made (frequency illusion).

The thing about desire is that the clues to achievement will continue to stand out in our lives. For all these things become added unto us, at the birth of desire (Luke 12:31).

So to come into the knowledge of how much income Independent Contractors that drove 18-wheelers generated ($100K a yr), served as only confirmation to what I had already been seeing around me. The only problem was, I was completely fearful of 18-wheelers.

(PAUSE) With that being said, now is a good time for me to share with you, a go to mantra of mines. For when times are tough, I remind myself of this, "God has not brought me this far to leave me (1 Corinthians 10:13)!"

For when God's light begins to shine, not only does your mind begin to project your potential, but your limitations are revealed as well.

Limitations can come in many forms, such as being faced with something you fear, lack of experience, lack of knowledge, lack of resources, etc. etc. I know this to be true, for I have dealt and still deal with different types of limitations along my journey.

The beauty of having faith is that faith allows the framework of your mind, to expand beyond your present circumstance, so that you may be able to see yourself living beyond your limitations (new viewpoint). And like the children of Israel (our mind) at the Red Sea (darkness), with the Pharaoh Of Egypt (present circumstance) breathing down their backs. God, who is an unlimited being, recognizes your faith and therefore provides a way (light) to get you to the other side.

To give you an idea to how this works in the modern-day, let's go back to the day I choose to walk into the light (idea) of being an Independent Contractor. What an indescribable moment that was...

Indescribable moments occur when thoughts of the past, present, and future all arise within the mind at the same time. In the sense of childbirth, the past arises as the parent reflects back on what their childhood was like. The present arises, as the conditions of the parent's present circumstance comes to mind. The future arises, as the parent ponders on what the future may hold.

Within the art of Hustling, an indescribable moment occurs, when we step into the light who we desire to be. For that light begins to shine on what I like to call the 3 G's. Gift (past), Grace (present), and Guidance (future).

The Gift is the talent or skill that God placed inside each of us at birth. In some form or fashion, we have been using this gift in our lives already, and now it will serve us as the vehicle that takes us to the mountaintop of our desired place. "I wish that all of you were as I am. But each of you has your own gift from God; one has this gift, another has that (1 Corinthians 7:7 NIV)."

Grace represents the Holy Spirit's assistance, and its purpose is to show us how to use our gift on the level of what we are desiring. "The Helper is the Spirit of Truth. The people of the world cannot accept him, because they don't see him or know him. But you know him. He lives with you, and he will be in you (John 14:17 ERV)."

Guidance represents Jesus, as the finished product of our desired state. The assistance that comes from the Holy Spirit is based on what our end goal is. "I admit that I haven't yet acquired the absolute fullness that I'm pursuing, but I run with passion into his abundance, so that I may reach the purpose that Jesus Christ has called me to fulfill and wants me to discover (Philippians 3:12 TPT)."

The first step to dealing with an indescribable moment or shall we say stepping into the light (idea) is to have faith that the light (idea) is good (Genesis 1:4). By having the faith that the idea (light) of being an Independent Contractor, was good for me, allowed God to continue to unfold my desire.

For God called the light (idea) good in Genesis 1:4 and then went into the next step of separating the light from the darkness. By me accepting that the idea (light) was good, my mind (God) then begin to project to me my potential (light), along with my limitations (darkness). If I had gone in the opposite direction and had no faith (doubt) in the idea (light). I would have shut down the whole operation and thus limited God's (my mind's) ability to go to the next step.

In the next step, the light (potential) that God separated from darkness, allowed me to see myself as already being an Independent Contractor (new viewpoint), making a $100K a year. While the darkness (limitations) revealed my fear of 18-wheelers, my lack of experience with driving a manual transmission, and the absence of resources to pay the $100 fee, that was due by the end of my first week in Truck Driving School (present circumstance).

The reason God separated my potential (light) from my limitations (darkness), is because it allowed me to have a choice in choosing faith or doubt. By choosing to have faith, to step into the light of being an Independent Contractor (guidance). God provided a way for me to get through the darkness, by releasing the Holy Spirit (grace) to assist me with the knowledge on how to overcome my limitations (darkness).

The Holy Spirit reminded me that God didn't give me a Spirit of fear but of one of power (2 Timothy 1:7). The power to be able to overcome and learn anything that I put my mind to (gift). By me facing my fears head-on. I discovered the presence of the Holy Spirit, and with the presence of the Holy Spirit, I learned that prior experiences don't really matter as much because the Holy Spirit will lead the way.

To better illustrate how this actually plays out in the modern-day world, let me take you through my first day behind the wheel of an 18-wheeler. I can admit, I was plenty fearful to get behind the controls of such a massive vehicle. Because at the time, the only thing that I knew about 18-wheelers, is that when they get into an accident, the truck is more than likely going to create total destruction to anything that it comes in contact with. But with me placing my faith in my new viewpoint (Independent Contractor) instead of my present circumstance of fearfulness. My potential was released, which enabled me to go beyond my fears and get behind the wheel.

Even though I was in a state of being fearful, from the moment I signed up for Truck Driving School and all the way down to the moment I was actually behind the wheel. The potential to get over my fear was inside me the whole time. It was just lying dormant until I put myself in a position to activate it.

Now let's go into my lack of experience because now I have to turn the key and operate a manual gear shift, something I have never done before successfully. The one time I have attempted to drive a manual gear shift before was a terrible experience in my eyes. For the car stalled on me as I was pulling out of a parking lot, and I ended up causing a mini traffic jam. I had no idea how to keep it from stalling out, I was just being a nice guy at the time, trying to help a friend out that was in a tight spot. Needless to say, I had to get out and push the car out of the way of traffic. I wasn't going to be able to push no 18-wheeler out of traffic. So coming into my new viewpoint, I was aware that my lack of experience existed.

After my first 5 attempts to start the truck and move the gear shift from neutral to first gear, the truck hadn't moved an inch. By this time, my classmates were laughing at me; my instructor was huffing and puffing at me. I could hear a person in the background saying, "Maybe you should try a different profession because you have to at least move the truck to make some money."

Needless to say, more laughter followed that comment, but I didn't let it bother me. I just keep encouraging myself (inner voice) and telling myself, "God hasn't brought me this far to leave me (acts of faith)!"

Then out of the blue, my Instructor said, "I'm tired of playing with you. We going to the highway, you either going to get it or you not." Then he put it into 4th gear and said "just drive, and I'll switch the gears." (PAUSE) Mind you; nobody has driven on the highway yet. We been at a abandon warehouse, driving around in a empty parking lot. Now he wants me to be the first, driving on the highway. I was shaken, I can't lie, but I never jumped out from behind the wheel (doubt). I just stayed the course and proceeded to drive towards the highway (Faith).

After five minutes of driving, the laughter had stopped, and that's when I realized for the first time in my life. That it doesn't matter what people think about me; the only thing that matters is what I tell myself (inner voice). Of course, other people can affect you, but only if you change your inner conversation to agree with what they're saying.

After 10 minutes of driving, my instructor said, "Well, at least you can drive; we can work on the shifting gears part. Pullover here and let somebody else get a turn on the highway." I was so relieved, not because he complimented me on my driving skills but because I didn't kill anybody lol. I'm so serious. Other students that day, may have learned how to shift the gears better or how to take the right angle on turning left. That's all fine and dandy, but I was just happy about not killing no one (changed a belief), and that was more than enough for me to build on.

The point is, that sometimes you will have to have your own experiences and let other people have theirs. Here's a bonus: Don't let someone else experiences affect your experience. For you have no idea what's going on inside their heads at the time. Were they choosing Faith or Doubt... Who knows!?!

Ways out of no way are created through faith! If you desire it and feel it's for you, go ahead and have your own experience.

Now let's recap my lack of experience adventure. Even though I had no prior experience with shifting gears. My gift to be able to drive showed up. The ability to shift gears is just another level within my gift of driving. There are levels to our gifts and the potential to reach those levels, lies dormant inside us until we put ourselves in a position to activate those potentials. Sort of like a student that goes from High School to College. For the college student lies dormant inside the high school student, until the student put themselves in position to activate their potential.

By the end of the week, I was shifting gears and driving with no assistance from my Instructor. For my focus was on what was to come (Independent Contractor) and not on what is (limitations). Having our sights (faith) on our new viewpoint, allows us to see ourselves living beyond our limitations, which is the key to overcoming limitations because the body is always following the mind!

Now let's go into my lack of resources adventure. We at the end of the week and the $100 fee that I haven't been having all week is due. The school secretary has been asking me every day this week, about this $100. Constantly reminding me that I can not come back to school on Monday if the $100 fee is not turned in by the close of business on Friday.

Now I don't know the inner workings of how money shows up out of nowhere, but this is apart of my testimony, so I have to share it. All I know is that I continued to go to school every day and worked on my craft of learning how to drive an 18-wheeler as if the money was just going to show up (acts of faith).

The reason I acted in this manner is because of what I had already seen transpire in my life. From seeing CDL opportunities floating all around me to being accepted into a truck driving school w/ paid tuition. Not to mention, just 4 days ago, I was scared to death of 18-wheeler's; now, I was at the point of driving one. I was walking through darkness (limitations), with my eyes (inner sight) on the light (potential). As the final day of the week approached, I was blessed with an opportunity to do a deed for someone, and for doing so without complaint, the person awarded me a $100 bill, which allowed me to pay the $100 fee and continue school (tear)!

As Hustlers, we must keep our newfound viewpoint (light) of ourselves, at the forefront of our minds because the outcome of our hustle (creation) depends on it. For we reap what we sow (2 Corinthians 9:6). In other words, the outcome of any given situation is determined by how we see that particular situation playing out (Guidance).

SCRIPTURES TO FIGHT WITH:

"The light shines in the darkness, and the darkness has not overcome it." ... **John 1:5 NIV**

"For the Spirit God gave us does not make us timid, but gives us power, love and self-discipline."... **2 Timothy 1:7 NIV**

"What you have said in the dark will be heard in the daylight, and what you have whispered in the ear of the inner rooms will be proclaimed from the roofs."... **Luke 12:3 NIV**

"God is faithful; he will not let you be tempted beyond what you can bear. But when you are tempted, he will also provide a way out so that you can endure it."... **1 Corinthians 10:13 NIV**

UNDERSTANDING GUIDANCE

Guidance is the direction that's provided by a guide.

*"And God made the firmament, and divided the waters which were under the firmament from the waters which were above the firmament: and it was so. And God called the firmament Heaven."... **Genesis 1:7-8 KJV***

There's an old saying that goes, "Everything that glitters is not gold!" That same saying can be said, for the numerous amounts of thoughts, that cycle in and out of our heads on a daily basis.

For we live in a world where our minds are constantly being bombarded with breaking news stories, can't miss t.v. shows, big-time sporting events, and the list goes on. So, in order to know which thoughts we should be holding on to or which thoughts we should be letting go of, we must ask ourselves this question... What is for me, and what is not for me!?!

The key to knowing what's for you and what is not, is to first identify what you're aiming for in life (end goal). There in comes the beauty of having and understanding your heart's desire. For the arrival of a desire, places your mind in a space of attainment. Within that space of attainment, you are able to see yourself having and enjoying the benefits of whatsoever you are desiring.

In the Bible, that space of attainment is known as Heaven, and the way to that space of attainment is often described as Jesus...

"In my Father's house are many mansions: if it were not so, I would have told you. I go to prepare a place for you. And if I go and prepare a place for you, I will come again, and receive you unto myself; that where I am, there ye may be also. And whither I go ye know, and the way ye know. (John 14:2-4 KJV)."

Within the art of Hustling, the many mansions in my Father's house represents the many different levels of desire, that are available for us to choose from. A place prepared for you, represents the mind framing into that particular desire, that we as individuals, have chosen to go after in our lives. The phrase, "that where I am, there ye may be also," represents the gravitational pull that the mind has over the body. For the body is always following the mind.

What the Bible is illustrating to us, is that when we go into that space of attainment and experience within our mind, what it's like to have the desire fulfilled (created). We are in actuality, activating the Jesus-like consciousness within us to guide us to the desired result (Heaven).

As we spend more and more time within that space of attainment (meditation/prayer). Our minds (Jesus) then begin to project (create) to us, the way to unite our earthly experience, with our heavenly desire. Thus the phrase, "the way you know."

The key to survival at this stage in the process of creating is to make a decision on what level of worth (money) you need, in order to obtain the level of desire you have.

As hustlers, it is vital for us to begin with the end goal (Heaven) in mind. For where we are desiring to end up at, determines the route we are going to take and the thoughts that we are going to need, to get us there. Remember, we are already masters at creating our future. We just have to let our past be our greatest teachers, as we move forward into our future.

To give you an idea of how our past, can be our greatest teachers on how to create... Let's take a common creation, such as being asked to go to the store.

No further instructions were given, we were just asked to go to the store (In the beginning). At that point, our minds would be all over the place. Thoughts would be seemingly coming out of nowhere (formless). Like, do we need to put on some more presentable clothing, or are we going through a drive-thru? Are we using a vehicle, or are we walking down the street? For during that brief moment, we have not the slightest clue on which store, we are being asked to go to or what we're being asked to pick up at the store (darkness).

Then let's say the person reveals that they would like for us to pick up a dozen of eggs from the supermarket (light). Now that we know what's being desired, our minds (Jesus-like consciousness) would then begin projecting unto us, how we are to go about uniting our heavenly desire of needing eggs, with our earthly experience of bringing the eggs home.

For instance, the type of clothing we need to wear is revealed, along with the best choice of transportation we should use. Even the path inside of the store is projected specifically to what we are desiring to have because the way to the eggs is not the same as the way to the toy section.

Also, notice that we have yet to take one foot out the door. We have only merged together within our imagination (mind), what we do have (earth), with what we don't have (heaven). Which then gave birth to the thoughts (light), on how to bring heaven to earth.

See that is what true guidance is, simply knowing what's being desired, creates the corresponding thoughts, that become the vision, that leads us to destiny!

Hustling With God

Through my experiences, God has shown me that the best way to bring a heavenly desire into an earthly experience is to breakdown what my mind (Jesus) is projecting and turn what the mind is projecting (creating) into individual desires and call them goals. For each goal, produces it's own thoughts. Thoughts that set us on course to bring Heaven to Earth.

*Below is an illustration of what it looks like, when one breaks down the framework of what the mind is projecting.

AND THIS SHALL COME TO PASS...
January 28, 2015 at 5:32 PM

AND THIS SHALL COME TO PASS...
I Will Progressively Get Better And Wiser Everyday as Tractor Trailer Driver

AND THIS SHALL COME TO PASS...
I Will Pass My CDL Driver's Course Test (Feb. 4th)

AND THIS SHALL COME TO PASS...
I Will Study And Pass My Driver's Endorsement (Feb. 3 & 4)
-Double Trailer
-Tanker
-Haz-Mat

AND THIS SHALL COME TO PASS...
I Will Get A Great Job Inside The Trucking Industry With Amazing Pay, With Amazing Benefits, With Amazing Training & Continue To Grow Positively As A Person, Spirit & As A Driv

AND THIS SHALL COME TO PASS...
I Will Get A Great Job Inside The Trucking Industry With Amazing Pay, With Amazing Benefits, With Amazing Training & Continue To Grow Positively As A Person, Spirit & As A Driver!

AND THIS SHALL COME TO PASS...
I Will Gain The Right Amount of Experience And Meet The Right Amount People To Gain Wisdom, Knowledge And Understanding on how to earn a Wealthy Income! ($100,000.00)

AND THIS SHALL COME TO PASS...
My Wife And I Will Buy Us A House That We And Our Family Can And Will Enjoy! That's Filled w/ All The Furniture And Appliance's Of Our Liking!

AND THIS SHALL COME TO PASS...
My Wife I Will Be Debt-Free (Jan. 1, 2016)

Sent from my iPhone

It is important to point out that I created this list of goals, while I was still going through Truck Driving School. At a time, when my new viewpoint of being an Independent Contractor, who produces $100K a year, was pretty much still just a dream. For I hadn't received my Commercial Drivers License yet, I hadn't even made a single dollar in the industry and my resources, rather cash or credit, were at an all-time low.

The reason that's an important point to magnify is because my list of goals were written down from a place I desired to be in life (new viewpoint) and not from the place I was at in life (present circumstance). <u>"Write the vision and make it plain... For the vision is yet for an appointed time, but at the end it shall speak, and not lie; because it will surely come... the just shall live by faith (Habakkuk 2:2-4 KJV)."</u>

As I look back on my journey, I didn't quite understand at the time why I would take my goal sheet out and re-read it back to myself numerous amounts of times throughout the day. But from where I stand today, I'm able to see how the daily intake of seeing a different reality for myself, disrupted the reality of my present circumstance (walking by faith). For I begin to notice that my mind and my life was beginning to frame, into what I was reading back to myself.

Case in point, I would wake up and go to Truck Driving School day after day and make what I thought to be, mistake after mistake, but in actuality, that was God's way of teaching me how to learn through my experiences. For I was learning from those mistakes and slowly but surely, my mistakes became less and less each day (Goal #1).

I went from having no time to study and if we being honest, not wanting to study. To willingly staying up late, putting in the extra time to understand the ins and outs of my CDL handbook (Goal #2&3).

My manners and my habits were changing right before my eyes. For I was continually placing my mind in the space of attainment by speaking life (faith) to what I desired (new viewpoint). "Death and life are in the power of the tongue: and they that love it shall eat the fruit thereof. (Proverbs 18:21 KJV)"

Now take a minute and witness that the first set of goals(#1-#3), were a list of things that I could control. Like, going to school every day and putting forth the effort to study. Then notice, that the next set of goals(#4-#5), were a list of the things that were completely out of my control. Like, getting a great job with amazing pay and meeting the right type of people to share with me the knowledge on how to do what I was attempting to do. For I couldn't hire or pay myself, nor could I control the type of people I meet in life, and even if I could, I still would not be able to make a person share with me the information that I needed to know. Those type of goals depends on God's support to be working behind the scenes.

So how do we get God to be working behind the scenes on our behalf? I'm glad you asked...

When we create goals, no matter how many goals we create. In the end, our goals will always be broken down into two different types of goals. Ones that you can bring to life through faith in yourself and the ones that can only come to life through the faith that you have in God. This is so because it falls back into the structure of the way the world was made (the blueprint).

For God made a Heaven in the mist of the waters (faith), which divided the faith that were below the

Heavens, from the faith which were above the Heavens (Genesis 1:7).

Heaven represents the place where God dwells, and faith is the thing that connects us with Heaven. That's why the Bible tells us, "Without faith, it is impossible to please God. (Hebrews 11:6)"

For instance, God is unable to grant me goal #4, a great job with amazing pay. If at first, I don't have the faith to complete goal #2, which is to pass my CDL drivers course test. For the goals above Heaven, are set into motion, the moment we start acting in faith, with the things that we can control on Earth.

Establishing a goal for yourself counts as an act of faith on Earth because it meets the definition in every way. "Faith is the substance of things hoped for, the evidence of things not seen (Hebrews 11:1 KJV)."

Now, to sum up this chapter on the understanding of guidance. It's important to know that within the art of Hustling, your level of guidance is determined by your level of desire. Without having a desire like goal #4, a great job with amazing pay. The odds of achieving a great job with amazing pay goes down substantially. <u>"For you have not because you ask not. (James 4:2)"</u>

I know this to be accurate information because in my past, I have unknowingly limited myself, by setting goals that were too low and then not recreating those goals, as they came to pass. The key to achieving God's guidance is to dream beyond your control. For that opens up the door, to that wonderful thing called Grace!

WORDS OF WISDOM

IF IT'S NOT THE THING YOU MEANT TO DO, IT'S THE THING THAT'S GOING TO BRING YOU CLOSER TO WHAT YOU MEANT TO DO.... T.D. JAKES

SCRIPTURES TO FIGHT WITH:

"Commit thy works unto the Lord, and thy thoughts shall be established." ... **Proverbs 16:3 KJV**

"And the Lord answered me, and said, Write the vision, and make it plain."... **Habakkuk 2:2 KJV**

"And all the time, you don't obtain what you want because you won't ask God for it!"... **James 4:2 TPT**

"What you say can preserve life or destroy it; so you must accept the consequences of your words."... **Proverbs 18:21 GNBDC**

UNDERSTANDING GRACE

Grace is the power that helps believers move from faith to faith. (Divine Assistance)

*"And God said, Let the waters under the heaven be gathered together unto one place, and let the dry land appear: and it was so."... **Genesis 1:9 KJV***

Have you ever bought a car or seen someone else with a car, that you have never heard of before? Then all of a sudden, it seems like you start seeing and hearing about that particular car, everywhere you go. The reason behind this sudden increase of attention is because that particular car has now entered into your space of awareness.

See, that particular car was always around, but due to your prior level of awareness, your senses never picked up on the presence of that car. But now that you are aware of that car's existence, your senses now alert you to whenever the car is brought up in conversation or whenever you see it in passing.

Within the art of Hustling, opportunities are all around us and there's no limit to what an opportunity can produce but often times many of our opportunities go unrecognized or don't reach their full potential. Due to our tendency, to knowingly or unknowingly, set the amount of worth that we see in ourselves too low.

The key to recognizing better opportunities and attracting the strategy to make the most out of those opportunities is to increase the amount of worth (money) that we see ourselves having. For when we do that, we create a space for God's grace to come into our space of awareness. To teach us how to elevate our hustle, to the level that we see ourselves being. And like new cars, whenever those opportunities are brought up in conversation or in passing, our senses will alert us to the presence of those opportunities.

Once again, the Bible provides us with a great illustration of how God's grace plays out in our spiritual lives. "But the Helper, the Holy Spirit, whom the Father will send in my name, he will teach you all things and bring to your remembrance all that I have said to you. (John 14:26 ESV)"

I hope that you are able to see the connection that's being bridged together between our last chapter on guidance and this chapter on grace. For in the above scripture, the phrase, all that I have said to you, is coming from the consciousness of Jesus, the guide to our destination. While the phrase, will teach you all things, is coming from the consciousness of the Holy Spirit, the provider of divine assistance. Both are on the same team, both are on a mission to help us succeed, and both are working in harmony with God's plan for our lives.

Now let's go back to our place in the blueprint on how we are meant to create. For God said, "Let the waters under the heaven be gathered together unto one place, and let the dry land appear: and it was so. (Genesis 1:9)"

The reason God included this step within the process of creation is so that we will undoubtedly be aware of the differences, in between following ourselves and following what the Holy Spirit is teaching us. For that is the question we will be asking ourselves the most... Is it me or is it God talking?

Remember in our previous chapter, we discussed how goals ultimately breakdown into two parts, ones that we are able to accomplish through faith in ourselves (under Heaven) and ones that we must rely on our faith in God to accomplish (above Heaven).

So when Gods says, "Let the waters under Heaven be gathered unto one place." That is a reference to how we as people, process the beginning of doing things. For when we begin a task, everything that we know about a particular subject (gathered together), naturally flows to the forefront of our minds (unto one place).

As the teachings of the Holy Spirit begins to flow into us, we will recognize those teachings as such because the teachings that the Holy Spirit will give (grace), are not in us in the beginning. For God separated the two when God made Heaven and divided the under from the above (Genesis 1:7)

The key to survival during this phase of creating is to learn how to move from faith to faith. That my friend is when the ever-present light of grace comes into the picture because we must be able to have faith in God, to follow the Holy Spirit's assistance, which flows to us from the waters (faith) that are above Heaven. The place were God dwells. "For Heaven is my throne, says the Lord. (Acts 7:49)"

Now let's take my journey, for example. In the Trucking business, it is a common belief that new CDL holders must start out driving over the road, in order to make some good money because the less experienced you are, the less money you will earn per mile.

Now notice goal #4, on the illustration provided in our previous chapter. I wrote out, that I desired to have a great job inside the trucking industry with amazing pay. To fully understand the words that I'm about to share, go back and visit the chapter labeled 'My Testimony.' For in that chapter, I shared with you my prayer to God, which detailed the type of hustle that I was looking for. One that will not only provide me with the type of money I desired to have but along with it, the type of peace, love, and joy that surpasses all of my understanding.

I remind you of that prayer, to share with you how every detail of our lives, is continuously being woven together, to fit into God's plan of bringing good into our lives.

My idea of having a great job with amazing pay is to have a job where I'm able to see my wife and my kids everyday while being able to be in the financial position, where my family will want for nothing in life. The common belief of having to drive over the road did not fit inside that frame because over the road driving, requires most drivers to be gone from home for weeks and weeks at a time. I don't know about other people's homes, but my house would not be at peace, with Daddy missing in action.

To add to that, I would not have experienced much joy, with my sons continually asking me, "When are you coming back home, daddy?" That may be fine with some people, and I'm not knocking them if they do, but that's not for me, and God knows that for God created me. I'm blessed to say that til this day, I have been working inside the Trucking industry for 4 years and counting, and have yet to spend more then 2 days away from home. Better yet on most nights, I'm at home.

My motive for sharing that insight is to let you know that it was not me that orchestrated such a move, but it was God's grace that guided me down such a path. In all honesty, if it was up to me. I would have made the sacrifice to go over the road and spend those weeks at a time away from home. For my financial situation at home, was just that bad, but God had other plans...

Before I attempt to explain the unexplainable grace of God. Let me first share with you some foretelling signs that you may be receiving God's grace.

Sign #1. You all of a sudden, come up with a brand new way of doing something, to something you already had prior experience with doing. The chances are that's the Holy Spirit teaching you.

Sign #2. You start thinking of an idea (light), and even though you have yet to tell a soul. You begin to overhear conversations on the need to have what you been thinking about. The chances are that's the Holy Spirit teaching you.

Sign #3. You began to get off track and distracted away from the path that you desire to be on. Then you begin to hear your own inner voice telling you, "get back on track, don't go that way, go this way." The chances are that's the Holy Spirit teaching you.

What it all boils down to is that faith comes by hearing, and it's not so much the outside voices that matter; it's all about what you and God say (Romans 10:17 KJV).

Now let's jump back into my journey. After having the faith to learn how to drive a 18-wheeler and after having the faith to take & pass the writing portion of the CDL test and after having the faith to take & pass the driving portion of the CDL test. God responded to my acts of faith by releasing the Holy Spirit to teach me how to go into the next phase of my vision (above heaven).

I was able to recognize those teachings as such because I was beginning to think in a way that I had never thought before. For instance, even though the world was telling me, I had to get a job driving over the road. The voice inside me was telling me to put my faith in the viewpoint of having peace, joy, and love and not in what the common belief was at the time. So I carried that thought out.

As a result, I later on overheard an opportunity, about a company that takes on newly licensed CDL holders, that have their drivers home every night. I immediately claimed that opportunity as mine (faith), checked in on the opportunity (act of faith) and was hired right away and as far as pay, I was making more money then I have ever produced before. I wasn't producing my desired income of $100K a year, but I could sense I was going in the right direction.

See, that's the beauty of receiving God's Grace. For God's grace puts you in position, to experience success along the way, while preparing you for what's to come.

With this opportunity, every part of goal #4 became a reality in my life. I received some amazing training that I still use to this day. I was offered top of the line health insurance for my family, which I took advantage of. My faith in God was increasing daily, as I was becoming more and more familiar with knowing the difference between God's voice (Holy Spirit) and my own.

With every day, came a lesson to learn. Lessons that involved learning from my mistakes and lessons that involved learning how to remain humble through my success.

To give you an idea of the type of lessons I was learning through my mistakes, would be when it was time for me to back the truck up to the entry point and drop the ramp. The ideal way of backing a truck to the entry point was to position the truck in a way that would allow the driver to back in and drop the ramp right at the door that the driver was going to be using to enter the building. The reason that this was an essential aspect of the job was because as a solo driver, each workday required several different deliveries to be made, so therefore the least amount of time and energy that a driver used per delivery, the better.

There were drivers working at this company that could position their truck in a way that would allow them to go from truck to building and be done in no time. Me on the other hand, I had a hard time not only positioning the truck. I also couldn't get my ramp nowhere near the door. So instead of going from truck to building, I oftentimes had to start out in the parking lot and would have to exert a lot more energy and time than other drivers to get my job done.

Every day and every delivery, positioning, backing, and dropping my ramp was a crucial part of my job. Every day and every delivery, I could hear the Holy Spirit's voice teaching me and encouraging me, on how to get better and better at the keys to being successful. Constantly reminding me that this too shall pass.

As time passed, I developed the skills to position, back in, and drop my ramp, right at the entry point of my choosing. For I had the faith to keep showing up every day and put the work in. Even through the time delays and the physical exhaustion of overworking myself, I stayed the course. As a result, my faith in the Holy Spirit and in my abilities, increase from one level to the next.

When it comes to examples of learning how to remain humble during times of success. A great example would be when I had to learn how to manage the increase in money, that I was now producing.

Trust me, money can be used to bring good into your life, and money can be used to bring destruction into your life. It's all about how you use it. God knew that, so therefore God sent me the Holy Spirit to teach me how to manage my money for the level that I was aspiring to be on.

The Holy Spirit taught me that it wasn't the money that needed to be managed but that it was me that needed managing. My individual problem with money was that I had my own secret agendas, with what I wanted to do with money. Of course, I wanted to be able to provide for my family, and I did provide for my family in every way possible, but for the first time in my life, I had money remaining over after taking care of my family.

The first lesson that I learned about managing myself is that my secret agendas did not fit in with God's plan for my life. For my secret agendas had plans of its own, which separated me from the plans of God.

In Matthew 6:24, the Bible talks about how no man can serve two masters. For either he will hate the one and love the other or else he will be loyal to one and reject the other.

I discovered that, in order for me to stay in line with God's plan. I had to remove myself from all the things that were pulling me away from God's plan because as I was moving further away and into the plans of my secret agendas, the less I was able to hear the voice of the Holy Spirit.

I later understood that the conflict was coming from the results that each plan was after. For my secret agendas plan was to take advantage of the opportunities that were beside me, while God's plan is to qualify me for the opportunities that are in front of me. The reason that I was beginning to hear the Holy Spirit's voice less and less is because I was no longer developing myself into something greater then I was, which voided the Holy Spirit's role in my life. For the waters above heaven, come to evolve us into something greater.

I know by experience that the walk of faith can seem to be intimidating at times because it puts you in a space of not knowing what's to come. Especially in the beginning stages, when you are unfamiliar with seeing darkness turn into light, but I want to remind you that God's Grace is always qualifying you for the journey ahead. By teaching you how to think from the level required to produce the amount of worth desired. For the amount of worth that you currently possess, does not require any outside assistance to produce, let alone any divine assistance. For you already have the experience and the know-how to produce what you currently possess (waters gathered together).

When we walk by faith with God. Know that no eyes have seen, no ears have heard, and no human mind has ever conceived, what God has prepared for those who love him (1 Corinthians 2:9). In other words, know that it's not intimidation that you may be experiencing, but it's preparation.

With that being said, God's grace may lead you down some paths that do not fulfill your amount of worth right away but know that it's definitely going to be a path that brings you closer to fulfilling your worth. So, don't be discouraged by the journey, for the journey is there to mold and shape your gift, to the level of your worth (viewpoint).

I know if I had been given my opportunity right out the gate. I would not have had the type of work ethic I needed to maintain the size of opportunity that God had prepared for me. But trust and believe, when my opportunity presented itself, I was beyond ready, and I haven't looked back ever since.

SCRIPTURES TO FIGHT WITH:

"So faith comes from hearing, that is, hearing the Good News about Christ (Your Dream)."... **Romans 10:17 NLT**

"Get rid of your old self, which made you live as you use to and put on the new self, which is created in God's likeness."... **Ephesians 4:22;24 GNBDC**

"Now unto him that is able to do exceeding abundantly above all that we ask or think, according to the power that worketh in us (grace)"... **Ephesians 3:20 KJV**

"Trust in the Lord with all your heart; and lean not unto your own understanding. In all your ways acknowledge him, and he shall direct your paths."... **Proverbs 3:5-6 KJV**

UNDERSTANDING DIVINE GIFTS

A gift is a natural ability or talent.

*"And the earth brought forth grass, and herb yielding seed after his kind, and the tree yielding fruit, whose seed was in itself, after his kind: and God saw that it was good."... **Genesis 1:12 KJV***

Throughout my childhood, I was fascinated with the idea of being like Johnny Appleseed. A guy that use to travel around the country, planting apple seeds, with the hopes of creating an orchard of apple trees. I even tried my hand at planting apple seeds throughout my front yard, hoping one day I'll be able to grow a tree of my own.

I remember being so amazed at how a single seed could become a tree that goes on to produce so many more apples.

Now that my childhood has come full circle in my life. I'm now able to see that the gifts God placed inside us all are very much like that apple seed. For our gifts are able to provide for us, on whatever level we desire to be on.

The key to survival during this phase of creating is to know that everything starts out small and then grows into what you need it to become.

From birth to now, we have been nurturing the gift God placed inside us, either through a collection of knowledge and/or by using the gift. I feel it's important to remind you that our journey in life doesn't begin when we start to go after the things we desire to have. Our journey in life begun at birth, when we were unknowingly becoming the person we are today.

One way to identify the gift inside of you, that was meant to assist you with producing wealth in your life, is to look back over your past and recognize the different types of ways you have been able to produce an income. For God is always strategically placing us in different situations and circumstances, to develop the gifts we've been given.

Now let's take a look inside of my journey for an example. One of the divine gifts that God placed inside of me is the ability to drive. There was a songwriter that once said, "There are levels to this." I reference that because during different stages of my life, I had one level of worth and at another stage, I had another level of worth. As I looked back over my own life, I discovered that each level of worth I had reflected itself in the amount of income that I was producing.

For instance, the first job I ever had was as a courtesy clerk, making $6.00 an hr. My job was to bag people's groceries up, push the grocery cart out to their vehicle, and assist them with putting their groceries inside. I went out and got that job because I was just looking for a way to start making some money. At the time, I didn't care how much money I was making; I was just happy with the fact that I was earning money. I didn't identify my worth to that job, but my worth reflected itself because I was just aiming for anything and anything I got.

The same thing happen with my second job; only this time, I was looking for a different way to make the money. My second job was as a Pizza Hut delivery driver, making $5.50 an hr. Plus tips. My job was to deliver pizza to those who wanted to enjoy their pizza at home or wherever else they so desired. Once again notice that the income reflected my worth because I was just looking for another avenue to make the money, not exactly an increase in funds but also notice the similarities, I was still driving something.

As my worth begins to increase, mostly due to life's responsibilities, such as having to take care of more people in my life, besides just myself. My paycheck ended up reflecting itself in that increase of worth, as I got on with a temp service that paid me $15 an hr.

Now let's fast forward to the place in my life when I asked God to show me how to hustle. As I mentioned before, God told me to "Try Faith!" So, for the first time in my life, I applied my faith to my worth. By declaring, I make $100K a year now. I didn't know how I was going to produce it, I simply just applied my size of faith to my amount of worth and what I discovered, is that the person that produces $100K a year was already inside of me. Just like the person who produced $6.00 hr. at my first job is still inside of me. I just had to bring it out. Now the tricky part is, I didn't know how to bring it out, but that's when faith comes in because with faith comes God's plan.

Now let's go back to our place in the blueprint on how we are meant to create. "And the earth brought forth grass, and herb yielding seed after his kind, and the tree yielding fruit, whose seed was in itself, after his kind: and God saw that it was good."... Genesis 1:12 KJV

The way this verse applies to us as Hustlers is that it reminds us that all of our potentials were placed inside of us at birth. The key phrases that I would like to highlight from that verse are "seed after his kind," "whose seed was in itself," and "saw that it was good."

Once again, I hope you are able to see the connection that's taken place between this chapter on our Gift and our last two chapters on Guidance and Grace. For this is that "indescribable moment" coming full circle.

On account of, that I could have applied for any job as my first job, and I definitely could have produced money in more ways than one (legally or illegally). There was something in me (God), that was guiding me and still guiding me to this day, to choose the type of setting that I'm suitable to produce in.

For example, I have never gone to a mechanic shop and tried to learn how to put a car back together. For God didn't place that gift within me, therefore there has never been any desire to go that route. Nice gift to have, but it's just not in me to do.

So when I say, an excellent way to identify the gift inside of you is to look within your past. It is because when God created the earth, God told the foundations of the earth, to go "after seeds of it's own kind" (Genesis 1:11). In this case, knowing where you come from will definitely help you with having an idea of where you are going to next.

Now let's address one of my favorite phrases, "whose seed was in itself." Like I said before, I discovered that the person that produces $100K a yr., was already inside me. I just had to find a way to pull it out of me.

I discovered this when God showed me the vision, on what I could become, and as I begin to walk the path to making that dream a reality. It became even more evident that I was just going to the next level of my gift when the experience that I had as a pizza delivery driver producing $5.50 hr. Started helping me as I was making my transition into becoming an Independent Contractor, who produces $100K a year.

A great example of how the experience of being a pizza delivery driver, helped me to become good at my job of delivering goods with an 18-wheeler, is by having the knowledge on how to make route adjustments when delivering to the same place more than once.

Similar to how there are certain customers that order pizza from their home quite often, there are certain warehouses and schools, that receive deliveries quite often, as well. By having the prior experience, on how to make route adjustments. It didn't take me long to figure out the best way to get to and from where I was going, which in turn afforded me the time and opportunity to work on my weakness of not being an experienced backer.

One thing that I want you to know is that God wastes nothing. Everything on Earth is made to help itself in some form or fashion, and we, as Creators and Hustlers, are no exception to that rule. **Know that your work in the Lord is never wasted (1 Corinthians 15:58 ERV).**

Now that I am a being, that produces over $200K a year and counting. I recognize that not only was the person that produces the amount of worth that I currently have, was already inside of me. I also recognize that everything that I have ever been in life is still in me too, and more importantly, everything that I desire to become in the future is already within me as well. For "whose seed was in itself" is in me!

Now let's move into the phrase that makes it all work, "saw that it was good." You can be given the greatest gift in the world, but if you don't see the value in that gift. That gift will remain useless to you.

With that being said, let's break down the fabric of what the phrase "saw that it was good" is showing us. First, notice the past tense use of the word 'saw' and 'was.' That is indicating to us that we should not only just see the good in having a gift but to see ourselves already using the gift, on the level that we desire to be on (Romans 12:3). Even when it actuality, we have no clue how to do so.

To better illustrate how you are able to implement this phrase into your individual life. Let's look at my journey as a case study. From the moment I created the desire to earn a $100K a yr., I held the vision of already doing so within my mind's eye, until the day it became a reality in my life.

All during truck driving school, I held the vision of producing $100K a yr. in my mind's eye. At the first job I got using my CDL, I held the vision of producing $100K a yr. in my mind's eye. Even though I wasn't producing $100K a yr., during those times, I was still firmly holding the vision of seeing my gift used to the level of my worth.

One may question, why would I continue to hold the vision, even though I wasn't producing the results that I desired to have?

And to that, I remind you of the key to surviving this phase of creating, which is to know that everything starts out small and then grows into what you need it to become.

I held on to the vision because I could see my gift growing right before my eyes. From overcoming the fear of being behind the wheel of an 18-wheeler and not having a clue on how to operate a manual transmission. To receiving my Commercial Drivers License and being hired on at a company, where I was producing more money than I had ever produced before.

To add to that, I also stayed the course because I could see God was bringing special people into my life. Special people that were on the same path that I was on. In Proverbs 18:16, the Bible tells us that our gift will bring us before great men. Great men are the men and women that are already doing what we desire to become. These great people show up in our lives, so that we may be given an opportunity to activate our faith.

When I say a chance to activate our faith, in this instance, I'm referring to an opportunity to step outside your comfort zone. In order to ask someone, "How am I able to get myself, to the level of where you are at in your life?"

I admit, this can be presented as a challenging moment because the moment requires you to humble yourself before another person and ask about something you don't have all the answers to.

One thing to keep in mind during this moment is to know that you are not putting your faith in that particular person, you are putting your faith in God to speak through that particular person. Meaning you don't take what that person says as gold. You hear that person out and then let the grace of God show you how their way, can help you in your life.

That my friend is why the idea of Faith is so important. For faith is the belief in things that you cannot see. Have faith that the dreams you have can become a reality. Have faith that you can provide for your family like you always dreamed of doing. Have faith that you can change your life into something better. Have faith that you can create that company that's been on your mind. For all these things are possible when you "Try Faith!"

Scriptures To Fight With:

*"A man's gift maketh room for him, and bringeth him before great men."... **Proverbs 18:16 KJV***

*"Thou hast been faithful over a few things, I will make thee ruler over many things."... **Matthew 25:23 KJV***

*"For I know the plans I have for you," declares the Lord, "plans to prosper you and not to harm you, plans to give you hope and a future."... **Jeremiah 29:11 NIV***

*"Don't think that you are better than you really are. You must see yourself just as you are. Decide what you are by the faith God has given each of us."... **Romans 12:3 ERV***

Bonus: PHASE II: MAINTAINING

Knowledge is the fact or condition of being aware of something.

*"You must not eat from the tree that gives knowledge about good and evil. If you eat fruit from that tree, on that day you will certainly die!"... **Genesis 2:17 ERV***

If you were to unknowingly, walk into the middle of a heart transplant procedure. The chances are, you will think that someone is in the process of being brutally murdered. For you will witness the insides of a person's body being exposed, their blood seemingly to be everywhere, and their heart laying over on a table somewhere. After gathering knowledge of what is exactly going on. You will begin to see that this is simply the process of what a successful heart transplant looks like.

While we are on our journey to creating who we desire to become, God will lead us down paths that to the normal eye will look like total destruction, but it's merely just what the process of success looks like.

The key to survival during this phase of creating is to release the knowledge of what you consider to be good and bad.

Case in point, at the first job I ever got using my newly acquired CDL. After 3 months of employment, I was fired from the company because I violated the company's rule, of having someone else ride with me. To the normal eye, that looks like what the hell are you doing, putting yourself in that position to mess up an opportunity that you worked so hard for. But to the one that's walking by faith, the reason I put myself in that position is because I was led by faith to do so.

The story goes like this; I took my brother to work with me one day because God told me to let my brother see me operating a manual gear shift. I resonated with God's idea of taking my brother to work with me because my brother was with me on the day that I attempted to drive a manual gear shift for the first time. He witness the stall outs, he witness how I said I'll never attempt to drive a manual gear shift again because of all the unsuccessful attempts and the complete embarrassment of blocking up traffic that we suffered through on that day.

For my brother to now become an eye witness to how we as people can overcome and learn something new. I was completely on board with God's plan. The problem was, I didn't have a clue about how my job would feel about me bringing my brother along for a ride. So I never asked anyone, eliminating the possibility of someone saying no to my brother coming along.

To make a long story short, the company found out that my brother went on the trip with me and fired me on the spot. Back at home, my wife wasn't too pleased about it and in fact, she was quite disappointed at me for putting my family in a tough situation. To the naked eye, it looks like I made a poor decision, but when you are walking by faith. The typical conditions don't apply, for God just kept telling me to stay faithful, stay positive, and everything is going to work itself out.

I would often remind my wife to remain faithful (to no avail), but how could I blame her. When I did step out of faith to see it through her viewpoint. It clearly looked like a devastating decision to make, but I didn't remain there. I jumped back into my viewpoint of earning $100K a year and begin to understand that God puts us in these situations because God's ways are higher than our ways, and God's thoughts are higher than our thoughts.

Not only was my brother exposed to the knowledge that we as individuals can overcome anything that we put our faith and effort into. Later on in his life, he gathered the faith to start hustling with God too. Since then, he has met the love of his life, started a family, and is on his way to leading his family to glory.

But that's not even the best part, not only was I back employed after a few weeks of being unemployed. My new company had a direct path to me becoming an Independent Contractor. By the end of the year, I was producing $100,000 in earned income. I was now living in a reality, that I had once only dreamed of.

To maintain faith in God along your journey, it may require you to walk alone sometimes and to let others come along on their own time. My Wife and I faith in God has grown substantially because we have been able to witness together; God's ability to make a way out of no way.

Just because God makes a way, doesn't mean the people around you are going to recognize the blessing as such. I have had many people close to me, dismiss my blessings as pure luck. But it wasn't meant for them to see it, it was meant for me to see. Stay faithful, stay worthy, and stay positive, and your blessings from Heaven will continue to flow your way!

SCRIPTURES TO FIGHT WITH:

"What shall we then say to these things? If God be for us, who can be against us?"... **Romans 8:31 KJV**